W9-AHK-043

Sue Hamilton

Published by ABDO Publishing Company, 8000 West 78th Street, Suite 310, Edina, MN 55439. Copyright ©2010 by Abdo Consulting Group, Inc. International copyrights reserved in all countries. No part of this book may be reproduced in any form without written permission from the publisher. ABDO & Daughters™ is a trademark and logo of ABDO Publishing Company.

Printed in the United States of America, North Mankato, Minnesota
112009
012010

 PRINTED ON RECYCLED PAPER

Editor & Graphic Design: John Hamilton
Cover Design: John Hamilton
Cover Photo: iStockphoto
Interior Photos and Illustrations: Alamy, p. 14, 18; AP Images, p. 17, 23, 24, 25; Getty Images, p. 7, 8, 9, 10, 12, 20, 27; iStockphoto, p. 1, 3, 4, 11, 15, 17, 28, 31, 32; National Geographic, p. 16, 29; Peter Arnold, p. 5, 13, 19; Photo Researchers, 6, 21, 22; Visuals Unlimited, p. 26.

Library of Congress Cataloging-in-Publication Data

Hamilton, Sue L., 1959-
  Attacked by a crocodile / Sue Hamilton.
    p. cm. -- (Close encounters of the wild kind)
  Includes index.
  ISBN 978-1-60453-929-5
  1. Crocodile attacks--Juvenile literature. 2. Crocodiles--Juvenile literature. I. Title.
  QL666.C925H36 2010
  597.98'2--dc22

                    2009045514

CONTENTS

ANCIENT REPTILE

Crocodiles have been on the planet for 200 million years. These powerful predators outlived the dinosaurs by nearly 65 million years. They are strong swimmers, with keen senses and muscular jaws. These highly adaptable lizards will eat nearly any kind of meat. They have no natural enemies, except humans.

American crocodiles are found in Florida, as well as Central and South America. However, Africa, Asia, and Australia have the greatest number of crocodiles. An African Nile crocodile grows as long as 20 feet (6 m) and weighs as much as 2,000 pounds (907 kg). Yet crocodiles can hide, nearly invisible, in less than one foot (.3 m) of murky water.

Crocodile attacks are common in areas where people and crocs regularly share the waterways. In Africa, the Nile crocodile is one of the most dangerous predators on the entire continent.

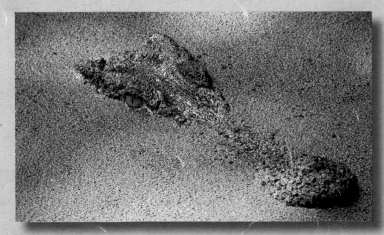

Right: A crocodile can remain nearly invisible in less than one foot (.3 m) of murky water.
Facing page: A Nile crocodile bursts out of a river in Kenya, Africa.

TEETH AND BITE FORCE

Crocodiles have an ample supply of sharp teeth, which they use for gripping and crushing their prey. They do not chew. Crocs have a large throat that allows them to swallow their prey whole or in big chunks. Their stomachs are filled with one of the strongest acidic fluids of any animal. Along with meat, this digestive fluid dissolves bones, shells, hooves, and horns.

The muscles a crocodile uses to open its jaws are relatively weak. Many people have seen a croc's mouth held shut with a person's bare hands. But the muscles a crocodile uses to *close* its jaws are incredibly powerful. In fact, a crocodile's bite force is one of the strongest of any animal. When a croc snaps its jaws shut, its prey seldom escapes.

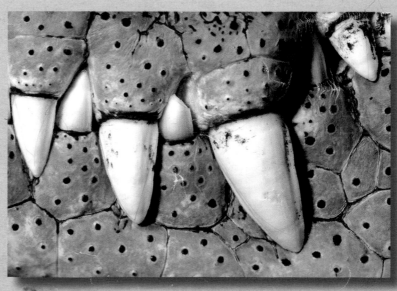

Right: A crocodile's bite force is one of the strongest of any animal.
Facing page: A Nile crocodile attacks a wildebeest in a river in Kenya, Africa.

SUCCESSFUL SENSES

Crocodiles are patient hunters. As they wait for prey in murky water, most of their bodies lie just under the surface. Their nostrils, eyes, and ears are located at the top of their heads, allowing them to float for hours if necessary. When prey wanders into range, crocodiles explode out of the water in a devastating surprise attack.

A full-grown, 450-pound (204-kg) crocodile can burst out of the water at 43 miles per hour (69 kph). On land, it can lift its body off the ground and "high walk" at speeds up to 14 miles per hour (23 kph). Crocs can only run like this for a short distance. Most healthy people can outrun a crocodile on land.

Above: Crocodiles can "high walk" at speeds up to 14 miles per hour (23 kph).

> **"Most crocodile attack victims never see the crocodile coming—they use surprise, not speed."**
> —Adam Britton, Florida Museum of Natural History

Crocs have a transparent third eyelid called a nictating membrane, which slides sideways across the eye. It allows the reptile to see while protecting its eyes during underwater attacks.

Crocs cannot see well underwater, but they easily see their prey on land, even at night. At the back of each eye is a reflecting layer called a tapetum. It allows crocs to see in low light, and makes their eyes appear to glow in the dark.

Crocodiles have a good sense of smell. They can sniff out a decaying animal from very far away. If they have the opportunity, they will scavenge a free meal rotting on shore and save their energy for another time.

An amazing fact about crocs is that they don't have to eat for long periods of time. Crocs store fat in their tails, and can go for a year without eating. But crocs aren't picky. They will eat whatever prey is available—bird, turtle, zebra, or human.

Right: A saltwater crocodile, with its eye opened underwater. *Facing page:* A group of crocodiles is attracted by a chunk of meat hanging overhead. Crocodiles have an excellent sense of smell.

NILE CROC ATTACK

South Africans share their rivers and dams with many animals, including ferocious Nile crocodiles. On February 23, 2006, 47-year-old citrus farmer Pieter Abrahamse rode his horse to a nearby reservoir for an evening swim. Before entering the water, he checked for dangerous hippos, but he forgot to look for signs of crocodiles. He waded in. After a few steps from shore, he was about stomach-deep in the water. Suddenly, he felt something bite him on his left hip. He quickly realized a Nile crocodile had picked him for dinner.

"I started to fight immediately," recalled Abrahamse. "So I hit him with my left arm, and then he went for my left forearm." The croc then tried to drown Abrahamse by pulling him underwater.

Above: A Nile crocodile on the shore of the Mara River, in Kenya, Africa.

> "What I didn't realize at the time was that it had let go because it had taken part of my left arm off."
>
> —Pieter Abrahamse, February 23, 2006, South Africa

Abrahamse frantically fought to regain his footing. As he stood up, he felt the crocodile lose its grip on his left arm. Abrahamse staggered towards shore and grabbed his horse's rope with his right hand. The intelligent animal instinctively fled the water, dragging his bleeding master to safety.

Once on shore, the farmer realized that the croc had not let him go—it had simply bitten off the lower part of his left arm. Abrahamse's hand, including his wedding ring, was now in the croc's stomach.

Abrahamse got home without bleeding to death. His wife drove him to a nearby hospital, where he eventually recovered. Despite his injury, he was lucky enough to live to tell the amazing tale of how he lost his wedding ring.

Above: Crocodiles kill and injure hundreds of people in Africa each year.

SALTY ATTACK

Australians are familiar with the saltwater crocodiles that live along the rivers, billabongs, and swamps of their northern coast. These huge lizards are commonly called "salties." Because of their fierce nature, warning signs are posted anywhere salties may call home. Unfortunately, crocodiles move around quite a bit, and occasionally one appears in an unexpected location. Wendy Petherick and her husband, Norm Moreen, discovered this the hard way.

Above: A croc warning sign in Kakadu National Park, Northern Territory, Australia.

On April 2, 2008, Wendy and Norm stopped at Australia's Litchfield National Park, a small recreational area near the town of Darwin, in the Northern Territory. The 36-year-old woman was washing her face on the edge of Walker Creek when an 8-foot (2.4-m) crocodile leapt out of the water. "I saw the croc out of the corner of my eye," she said. But before she could react, her legs were in the creature's jaws, and she was being dragged into the river.

Terrified that the croc would soon begin a death roll, Wendy screamed and tried to pry open its jaws. A death roll is when a croc bites down on its prey and spins around and around. This weakens the prey, sometimes drowns it, and often tears off limbs. Luckily for Wendy, her husband Norm didn't give the croc time to start rolling.

Above: A saltwater crocodile swimming underwater.

> ## "We got away because we both fought back. If my husband hadn't been there, I would have been killed."
>
> —Wendy Petherick, April 3, 2008, Litchfield National Park, Australia

---

Seeing his wife in danger, Norm immediately leapt on top of the reptile, searching for the croc's eyes. "He poked his eyes and the croc freed me, and Norm just pushed me toward the side of the bank and both of us just got out of the water," said Wendy.

The croc swam off. Wendy was taken to a nearby hospital, where she was treated for nine puncture wounds on her legs and a deep cut to one of her fingers. Norm suffered minor scratches.

Wendy is quick to credit her husband for saving her life, but Norm shrugs off the attention. "I just jumped on top of it," he said. "There was no time for fear. It was all common sense." After the attack, local park rangers set traps in hopes of capturing the dangerous crocodile.

Above: Wendy Petherick.

Above: A salty with blood on its teeth.

INDIA CROC ATTACK

The city of Vadodara, India, has a population of more than 1.6 million people. It sits near the Mahi, Narmada, and Vishwamitri Rivers. The people of the city share their abundant waterways with a large number of crocodiles. This sometimes leads to unfortunate and terrifying encounters.

On April 19, 2005, Chanchal Baria was at a village ghat, a place where people go to wash and bathe. She took her clothes down the steps to the water and began washing them. Suddenly, a seven-foot (2-m) crocodile erupted from the cloudy water, grabbing the 45-year-old woman.

Above: Women in India washing clothes at a riverbank.

The croc immediately tried to pull Baria down and drown her. But the woman fought back, grabbing a boulder to keep herself from being taken. Her screams attracted bystanders, who threw rocks at the croc. "Reluctantly, the animal threw her to one side and disappeared in the murky waters," said Mafat Parmar, one of her rescuers.

Baria survived, and was taken to a local hospital with deep bites. The attack greatly concerned the villagers. Unfortunately, it wasn't the first time a crocodile had attacked someone. Ten days earlier, another man received bites on his back and waist when a croc attacked him from behind.

Crocodiles are intelligent. They learn routines. They hear noises like footsteps or splashing, and make the connection that their "prey" is making those sounds. It is important for people to be extra cautious, and never approach a known croc area alone.

Above: Many villagers in India must share the rivers with crocodiles.

> "By the time I called for help, the animal had started gnawing on her."
> —Saroj, Victim's Friend, April 19, 2005, Vadodara, India

Above: A marsh crocodile suns itself on a riverbank in India.

A crocodile has thick, protective skin. Its back is covered in bony scales called scutes. This thick exoskeleton can even repel bullets. However, the underside of a crocodile is softer and less armored. The throat and belly are where a veterinarian shoots tranquilizer darts to put the animal to sleep. Of course, as one veterinarian now knows, it's best to wait until the anesthetic has taken full effect before placing one's hand near the reptile.

On April 11, 2007, veterinarian Chang Po-Yu, of Taiwan's Shoushan Zoo, needed to remove a tranquilizer dart from the neck of one of the zoo's Nile crocodiles, and then give the animal some medication. The croc had not eaten for a month.

It seemed like a typical day for a veterinarian. But the 440-pound (200-kg) croc had other plans. When 38-year-old Chang reached into the cage to pull the dart, the croc turned on the vet, biting off his left forearm.

Right: Crocodiles have a thick exoskeleton that can sometimes even repel bullets.

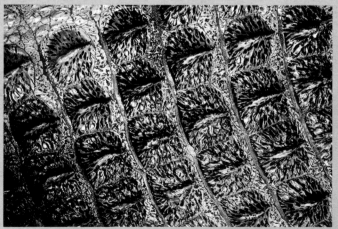

> "The arm slipped from the animal's jaw and bounced across the ground."
> —Zoo Employee, April 11, 2007, Shoushan Zoo, Taiwan

Above: Veterinarian Chang Po-Yu's forearm in the jaws of a Nile crocodile.

Chang was immediately rushed to a nearby hospital. Meanwhile, the Nile crocodile sat in his cage, with Chang's forearm in its mouth. To retrieve the forearm, another zoo official fired a gun at the reptile. Unhurt but startled, the croc dropped the forearm and moved away. "It probably was shocked and opened its mouth to let go of the limb," said zoo official Chen Po-Tsun.

The forearm was quickly retrieved from the cage. It was sealed in a bag, placed in a cooler of ice, then rushed to the hospital. Chang underwent more than seven hours of surgery to successfully reattach his forearm.

Captive crocodiles, even when partially sedated, can still be dangerous creatures. People must respect them or face the consequences.

Above: A security guard shoots and startles the crocodile, which releases Chang's forearm.

"No, I don't have any hard feelings for him. He's a croc. That's what croc's do."
—Chang Po-Yu, referring to the crocodile that bit off his forearm, Shoushan Zoo, Taiwan

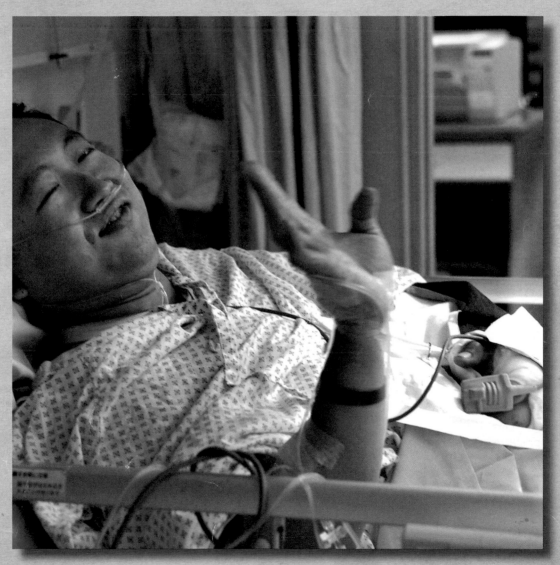

Above: Veterinarian Chang Po-Yu underwent a seven-hour reattachment surgery after a 440-pound (200-kg) Nile crocodile bit off his left forearm. Doctors at the Kaohsiung Medical University Hospital in Taiwan reconnected most of the forearm's blood vessels, nerves, and muscles. Chang may regain as much as 80 percent of his hand's function.

AVOIDING A CROC ATTACK

Crocodiles prefer fish or deer for their dinner, but a human at the shoreline is meat-on-a-stick to the reptiles. Because crocodiles are so fiercely protective of their territory, and will take the opportunity to eat whatever comes their way, they are a dangerous predator that humans must respect.

While there are a large number of attacks and killings in Africa and Asia, even American crocodiles found in South America and the southern United States present a danger.

Above: An American crocodile swims through a marsh in Sanibel Island, Florida.

To stay safe in known crocodile areas, keep away from the water. This advice sounds simple, yet attacks regularly occur in crocodile-infested waters. Avoid walking near the shore or entering water at dusk or at night. Crocs actively hunt during this time. They can leap out of the water and grab you. At minimum, stay 15 feet (4.6 m) away from the shore. If you do cross paths with a crocodile, turn and run away as fast as you can. Most healthy people can outrun a crocodile on land.

Do not dangle your arms or legs over the side of a boat or dock. Crocs have been known to attack boats, and they won't hesitate to leap up and bite tasty limbs dangled in front of them.

If camping in an area where crocodiles have been spotted, do not leave food or bait in the open. Do not clean fish near the shoreline. Leaving blood and entrails is like sending a croc a party invitation to come and eat.

Even if no warning signs are posted, ask before assuming an area is safe. Whether in Australia or Florida, it is best to avoid fending off a crocodile. Remember, these reptiles have survived for millions of years because they are powerful, fast, and smart.

Above: Make sure an area is safe before swimming.

SURVIVING AN ATTACK

What if a crocodile attacks you? Survivors all report that the reason they are alive is because they, and probably other people around them, fought the crocodile with everything they had. Stones, fists, a camera—use whatever you have to jab at the fierce reptile. Go for its eyes or its snout.

Some desperate victims have shoved their arms deep into the reptile's throat. At the back is a sensitive flap called the glottis, which leads to the trachea, a tube that conducts air to the croc's lungs. The glottis helps keep water out of the croc's lungs when it is submerged. Punching the back of the throat can panic the reptile, making it open its mouth. The danger in trying this is that the reptile may also close its mouth around the person's arm, biting off the limb. However, when desperate times call for desperate actions, there is a chance this will work.

Right: Some desperate victims have shoved their arm deep into a croc's throat. Punching the back of its throat can panic the reptile, making it open its mouth and free its prey.

If you are grabbed near the shore, fight to stay out of the water. The croc will try to death roll you, drowning you or ripping off limbs. A croc can easily hold its breath for 20 minutes. Most humans have a tough time holding their breath for a minute.

The best bet for survival against this powerful predator is to avoid the encounter altogether. Stay alert, but be prepared to scream, yell, and fight when attacked by a crocodile.

Above: If you are attacked by a crocodile, be prepared to fight for your life.

GLOSSARY

ACIDIC

Something with the harsh, corrosive properties of acid. Fluids in the stomach are acidic in order to digest food.

BILLABONG

A dead-end pool formed either as an offshoot of a main river or by water flowing into an area during flooding.

DEATH ROLL

When a crocodile bites down and holds its prey, then rolls itself and the victim over and over in the water in order to quickly disorient and drown the victim.

DECAY

When bacteria and fungi cause a living thing to rot or decompose.

DIGESTIVE FLUID

The watery-like fluid inside an animal's stomach that works to digest food.

EXOSKELETON

A hard external skeleton made of bones or shells found on insects (spiders), as well as crustaceans (crabs and lobsters), and reptiles (turtles, crocodiles, and alligators). This hard exterior helps support and protect the animal. Reptiles, such as crocodiles, have both an exoskeleton and an endoskeleton inside their body.

GHAT

In India, a flight of steps that leads down to the bank of a river, where people go to wash.

INSTINCT

A way to behave in certain situations that is known, not learned.

NICTATING MEMBRANE

A thin, transparent, skin-like flap that is an extra eyelid designed to protect a crocodile's eyes when it is hunting prey.

TAPETUM

A mirror-like layer at the back of a crocodile's eye that reflects light and allows the reptile to see at night. It also causes a crocodile's eyes to glow in the dark.

INDEX